Gracefully ROOTED

QUIET THE MIND AND HEAL THE SOUL: RIDE THE WAVE

30 Days of Self-Empowerment:
A Journal Companion for Women

FELICIA WILLIS

Dedication

To my devoted husband, Jonathan Willis, who challenges me to reach my full potential in family, business and ministry. You have been an inspiration on this journey.

To my loving parents, Noel & Joann Dixon, who taught me the value of perseverance and the power of dreams. My consistent supporters who have been a part of every milestone in my life.

To my precious children, Jon II, Jami, and Journi, who are the reason behind every word I write and every step I take. Who have taught me to self-explore new dimensions of myself and force me to activate my super powers.

And to all the women whose lives this book may touch, may you find strength, hope, and the spark to ignite your own extraordinary story.

Dedication

Dedication to my sweet Angel, the one and only, Mother Claudine Austin,

Your belief in me, even when I doubted myself, has been a driving force behind my success. Your guidance has not only enriched my knowledge but also deepened my understanding of being a Woman in Ministry.

I am profoundly grateful for the countless hours you spent patiently answering my questions, offering valuable insights, and challenging me to think beyond my limits. Your dedication to my growth was nothing short of extraordinary.

This book would not have been possible without your mentorship and the invaluable lessons you imparted. These two principles you left with me continue to guide my life and ministry: "Everything you do, do it in the spirit of EXCELLENCE" and "motherhood and marriage is not for wimps" As I embark on this journey, I carry with me the wisdom you've shared and the confidence you've instilled in me.

Table of Contents

To all the extraordinary women,

I am delighted to welcome you to this transformative 30-day journey of self- empowerment through our journal companion. As the founder of Wellness 365, I'm eager to introduce you to wellness concepts that have profoundly impacted my life in ways that are beyond words. This endeavor is more than just a collection of pages, but I t' s an opportunity to embark on a deep and meaningful journey of self-discovery, growth, and empowerment.

Each day, as you put pen to paper and pour your thoughts onto these pages, remember that you are embarking on a journey of self- reflection and self-empowerment. To initiate our real-life application process, please join in and continue embracing these small challenges in your daily life, and witness how they can create significant positive changes. Our goal with this journal companion is simple yet profound: to help you recognize the power within you and to equip you with the means to unleash that potential to its maximum capacity.

Throughout these 30 days, I encourage you to be authentic and honest with yourself. Let your journal be a sanctuary where you can express your deepest thoughts, dreams, and aspirations. Embrace your vulnerabilities as strengths and your challenges as opportunities for growth. As you move through this journal, you will uncover your inner strengths, clarify your goals, and tap into your potential. I hope that by the end of this 30-day experience, you will not only have a deeper understanding of yourself but also a renewed sense of purpose and confidence.

Ultimately, I want you to emerge from this moment feeling empowered, inspired, and ready to take on the world with newfound clarity and determination. This journal is your companion, your confidant, and your guide, but the real transformation lies within you. So, here's to the incredible journey ahead! Let your words flow freely, your thoughts flourish, and your spirit soar. You are capable of achieving greatness, and I believe wholeheartedly that this 30-day journal companion will be a valuable steppingstone on your path to self- empowerment.

Gracefully Submitted,

Felicia Willis

Hey Sis Hey,

This letter, as you know, means a lot to me. This dimension of health is the very foundation of which my life is governed. I want to share a heartfelt message about the significance of your spiritual wellness.

Each individual will experience their own spiritual walk and encounter with God on their journey towards spiritual growth. Each walk, guided by God' s grace, prayer, and devotion, is an amazing path that can illuminate your life in beautiful and transformative ways.

As we navigate our individual assignments and obstacles, my hope and prayer for you is that you find a deep and abiding connection with God. May your devotion be a source of strength during challenging times, a wellspring of gratitude in moments of abundance, and a guiding light in the darkest of places.

Through prayer and communion with God, may you discover the peace that surpasses all understanding, a profound sense of purpose rooted in faith, and a love that knows no bounds. Embrace this journey with an open heart, for in it lies the opportunity for spiritual awakening and profound growth.

Remember that your spiritual well-being is a personal and unique experience, shaped by your relationship with God. Cherish it, nurture it, and let it be a constant source of inspiration and guidance in the beautiful tapestry of life that God has woven for you.

Gracefully Submitted,

Felicia Willis

Spark your inner light and witness the world around you glow.

- F . E . W

DAY 1: FULFILLING A PURPOSEFUL LIFE

FAITH IN CHRIST

At the core of a Christian woman's life is her relationship with Jesus Christ. A fulfilling life involves a deep and personal connection with Him, relying on Him for guidance, strength, and salvation.

LIVING ACCORDING TO GOD'S WILL

Seeking and discerning God's will is essential. This means being open to God's direction and guidance in all aspects of life, whether it's in relationships, career choices, or personal growth.

SERVICE AND COMPASSION

A fulfilling life often includes a commitment to serving others and showing compassion. Christian women are called to love their neighbors as themselves, demonstrating kindness, empathy, and generosity to those in need.

FAMILY AND RELATIONSHIPS

Nurturing loving and healthy relationships, including family, friends, and the church community, is important. Christian women often find fulfillment in building strong, supportive relationships and providing love and care to their families.

PERSONAL GROWTH AND SELF-CARE

Self-improvement and self-care are essential components of a fulfilling life. This includes growing spiritually, emotionally, and intellectually, taking care of one's physical and mental health, and nurturing personal talents and interests.

LIVING WITH INTEGRITY

Upholding Christian values and principles in daily life is crucial. Living with integrity means being honest, trustworthy, and demonstrating moral character in all interactions and decisions.

DAY 1: FULFILLING A PURPOSEFUL LIFE

PURPOSEFUL WORK

Finding purpose in one's vocation or career is significant. Christian women often seek to use their skills and talents in ways that align with their faith and contribute positively to society.

PRAYER AND WORSHIP

Regular prayer, worship, and engagement with Scripture help maintain a strong spiritual connection and a sense of purpose in a Christian woman's life.

FAITHFUL STEWARDSHIP

Being responsible stewards of the resources and blessings God has provided, including time, talents, and material possessions, is a key aspect of living purposefully.

SERVING IN MINISTRY

Active involvement in the ministry of the church, such as teaching, counseling, or leading, can bring a sense of fulfillment by contributing to the spiritual growth of others.

Ultimately, a fulfilling and purposeful life as a Christian woman involves seeking God's guidance, continually growing in faith and love, and living in a way that reflects Christ's teachings. It's a lifelong journey of faith, service, and discipleship that brings deep joy and fulfillment.

Felicia's Grace Gems

REFERENCE SCRIPTURE | PROVERBS 19:21 (NIV)

Many are the plans in a person's heart, but it is the Lord's purpose that prevails.

PRAYER GUIDE | UNVEILING YOUR CALLING

Ask God to reveal your calling and the specific ways in which you can make a positive impact on the world and fulfill your purpose.

APPLICATION

Reflect on your vision of a fulfilling and purposeful life. What steps can you take to move closer to that vision?

DAY 2: SENSE OF PEACE

Having a deep sense of peace and inner calm as a Christian woman involves experiencing a profound tranquility and contentment that is rooted in your faith in Christ. Here are some key aspects of what this can mean:

TRUST IN GOD

Peace and inner calm often come from placing your trust in God. As a Christian woman, you trust that God is in control of your life and that His plans are for your good (Jeremiah 29:11). This trust allows you to surrender your worries and anxieties to Him.

PRAYER AND MEDITATION

Seeking and discerning God's will is essential. This means being open to God's direction and guidance in all aspects of life, whether it's in relationships, career choices, or personal growth.

FAITH IN GOD'S PROMISES

Believing in the promises of God, such as His promise to never leave or forsake you (Hebrews 13:5) and His promise of peace (John 14:27), can bring a deep sense of security and tranquility.

CULTIVATING A GRATEFUL HEART

Expressing gratitude for God's blessings, both big and small, can lead to inner calm. Recognizing His presence in your life and acknowledging His goodness fosters a sense of contentment.

LETTING GO OF CONTROL

Surrendering control of your life to God can be challenging but is key to inner calm. As a Christian woman, you understand that you are not in charge, and you find peace in yielding to God's guidance.

DAY 2: SENSE OF PEACE

LIVING IN ALIGNMENT WITH CHRISTIAN VALUES

Following Christian values, such as love, kindness, and forgiveness, promotes inner calm. When you live according to these principles, you experience peace in your interactions with others and within yourself.

ACTS OF SERVICE

Serving others, whether through volunteering or acts of kindness, can bring a sense of fulfillment and inner peace as you follow Christ's example of selflessness.

MINDFULNESS AND PRESENCE

Being present in the moment and practicing mindfulness can help you tune into God's presence in everyday life, fostering inner calm and an awareness of His peace.

In essence, having a deep sense of peace and inner calm as a Christian woman involves grounding yourself in your faith, trusting in God's sovereignty, and actively seeking His presence and guidance in your life. It's a continuous journey of spiritual growth and reliance on God's peace that transcends circumstances.

Felicia's Grace Gems

REFERENCE SCRIPTURE | PHILIPPIANS 4:6-7 (NIV)

Do not be anxious about anything, but in every situation, by prayer and petition, with thanksgiving, present your requests to God. And the peace of God, which transcends all understanding, will guard your hearts and your minds in Christ Jesus.

PRAYER POINT | PEACE OF MIND

Pray for inner peace and tranquility. Ask God to calm anxious thoughts and help you find mental rest.

APPLICATION

Write about a moment when you experienced a deep sense of peace and inner calm.

DAY 3: SELF COMPASSION 101

Self-compassion is an important concept that can benefit individuals from various backgrounds, including Christians, during challenging times. It involves treating oneself with the same kindness, understanding, and forgiveness that one would offer to a friend facing difficulties. Here's why self-compassion is valuable for Christians and how they can practice it during tough times:

BIBLICAL SUPPORT

Christianity teaches the importance of love, compassion, and forgiveness. Christians are encouraged to love their neighbors as themselves (Matthew 22:39) and to forgive others as God forgives them (Ephesians 4:32). Self-compassion aligns with these principles by urging individuals to extend the same love and forgiveness to themselves.

REDUCES SELF-CRITICISM

During challenging times, it's common for people to become self-critical and blame themselves for their circumstances. Self-compassion helps Christians avoid this trap by promoting self-kindness instead of self-judgment.

EMOTIONAL RESILIENCE

Self-compassion can enhance emotional resilience. It allows Christians to acknowledge their suffering without self-pity, which can help them bounce back from adversity with greater strength and faith.

ENHANCES EMPATHY

When Christians practice self-compassion, they may find it easier to extend empathy and compassion to others. This aligns with the Christian value of loving one's neighbor and can lead to more meaningful relationships.

DAY 3: SELF COMPASSION 101

To practice self-compassion during challenging times as a Christian:

SELF-REFLECTION

Take some time to reflect on your thoughts and emotions. Recognize and acknowledge any self-criticism or negative self-talk that may be present.

SPEAK KINDLY TO YOURSELF

Replace self-criticism with self-kindness. Use positive and compassionate self-talk, similar to how you would encourage and console a friend.

FORGIVENESS

Practice self-forgiveness for any mistakes or shortcomings you may have encountered. Remember that God's forgiveness is available, and you can accept it for yourself as well.

SET REALISTIC EXPECTATIONS

Understand that everyone faces challenging times, and it's okay to have limitations. Set realistic expectations for yourself and avoid perfectionism.

GRATITUDE

Cultivate an attitude of gratitude. Focus on the blessings in your life, even during difficult times, to maintain a positive perspective.

PROFESSIONAL HELP

If necessary, don't hesitate to seek help from a mental health professional or counselor. Christianity encourages seeking help when needed, just as you would seek medical assistance for physical ailments.

DAY 3: SELF COMPASSION 101

Incorporating self-compassion into your Christian faith can help you navigate challenging times with greater emotional well-being, resilience, and a deeper connection to your faith. It allows you to embrace God's love and extend it to yourself, empowering you to better love and serve others.

Felicia's Grace Gems

REFERENCE SCRIPTURE | EPHESIANS 2:10 NIV
For we are God's handiwork, created in Christ Jesus to do good works, which God prepared in advance for us to do.

PRAYER POINT | SELF-COMPASSION
Ask for the ability to love and accept yourself as you are, and to show yourself the same compassion and kindness that God extends to you.

APPLICATION

Reflect on the importance of self-compassion and how you practice it during challenging times?

Hey Sis Hey,

In this message, I will share thoughts on the benefits and spiritual importance of maintaining mental wellness. There is a deep spiritual aspect to mental wellness that is not often discussed in our communities. Your mind is the gateway to your inner self, your soul, and your connection to everything around you. When your mind is at peace, healthy and whole, you can explore the depths of who you are and find inner harmony, all while experiencing a sense of oneness with the world around you.

It is important to note that your mental health and well-being, is just as important as your physical health. As you feed your body with nutritious food and exercise, you must also feed your mind. Mental wellness is not optional, it' s a necessity for a fulfilling and purposeful life.

When you prioritize your mental health, you open the door to a multitude of benefits. A healthy mind allows you to cope better with life' s challenges, manage stress effectively, and build resilience. I t empowers you to make wise decisions, strengthen relationships, and pursue your goals with clarity and determination.

At a recent appoint with my primary care physician, she stressed the importance of meditation, mindfulness, and self-reflection as powerful tools that can help you cultivate mental wellness and deepen your spiritual journey. They allow you to quiet the noise of everyday life, tune into your inner thoughts and discover sense of purpose and meaning.

I urge you to make mental wellness a priority in your life. This will enhance your well-being but also tap into the spiritual realm of your life. Your mental health is a precious gift, and when you care for it, you open the door to a more enlightened and fulfilling experiences.

Remember that it' s okay to seek support when needed. Seeking guidance from a therapist, counselor, or mentor can be a transformative step towards better mental health. Don' t hesitate to reach out to those who can assist you on this journey.

Gracefully Submitted,

Felicia Willis

DONT ALLOW ANYONE TO DIMINISH YOUR INNER SHINE

- F.E.W

DAY 4: PRIORITIZING YOUR MENTAL HEALTH

Prioritizing wellness as a Christian is essential because it aligns with the teachings and values of Christianity and promotes overall well-being, allowing individuals to better serve God and others. Here are some reasons why prioritizing wellness is important for Christians:

HONORING THE BODY AS A TEMPLE

Christians believe that their bodies are temples of the Holy Spirit (1 Corinthians 6:19-20). Prioritizing wellness means taking care of the physical, mental, and emotional aspects of oneself, thereby honoring God's creation.

STEWARDSHIP

Christians are called to be good stewards of the resources God has entrusted to them, including their health and well-being. Taking steps to maintain good health is a responsible way to fulfill this stewardship.

EFFECTIVE SERVICE

A healthy and well-balanced individual is more capable of serving others effectively. When Christians prioritize wellness, they have the physical and mental energy to minister, help, and support others in need.

MENTAL AND EMOTIONAL HEALTH

Wellness includes mental and emotional health. Prioritizing these aspects can help Christians cope with stress, anxiety, and the challenges of life. It enables them to maintain a positive attitude and trust in God's plan, even during difficult times.

SETTING AN EXAMPLE

By prioritizing wellness, Christians can set a positive example for their communities and inspire others to do the same. Leading a healthy lifestyle can influence others to make positive changes in their own lives.

DAY 4: PRIORITIZING YOUR MENTAL HEALTH

LONGEVITY AND QUALITY OF LIFE

A commitment to wellness can lead to a longer and more fulfilling life. This allows Christians to continue their service and ministry for an extended period, impacting more lives in the process.

REFLECTING GOD'S LOVE

Prioritizing wellness reflects the love and care that God has for His children. By taking care of themselves, Christians demonstrate gratitude for God's love and His desire for them to live abundant lives.

In summary, prioritizing wellness as a Christian is not only compatible with one's faith but also enhances one's ability to live out the Christian values of love, service, and stewardship. By caring for their physical, mental, and emotional health, Christians can better fulfill their purpose and serve God and others more effectively.

Felicia's Grace Gems

REFERENCE SCRIPTURE | MATTHEW 11:28-30 (NIV)

Come to me, all you who are weary and burdened, and I will give you rest. Take my yoke upon you and learn from me, for I am gentle and humble in heart, and you will find rest for your souls. For my yoke is easy and my burden is light.

PRAYER POINT | EMOTIONAL AWARENESS

Pray for increased self-awareness regarding your mental health, emotions, and thoughts. Ask for the ability to recognize when you may need support or self-care.

APPLICATION

What does wellness mean to you, and how do you prioritize it in your life?

DAY 5: THE POWER OF CELEBRATION

Celebrating your achievements is important for several reasons, and it can have a positive impact on your well-being, motivation, and overall life satisfaction. Here are some key reasons why celebrating your achievements is essential:

BOOSTS SELF-ESTEEM

Celebrating your achievements helps boost your self-esteem and self-worth. Recognizing and acknowledging your accomplishments can make you feel proud of yourself and your capabilities.

MOTIVATION AND GOAL SETTING

Celebrating your achievements provides motivation to set and pursue new goals. When you experience the satisfaction of reaching a milestone, you're more likely to be motivated to set and work toward future objectives.

POSITIVE REINFORCEMENT

Celebrating achievements reinforces positive behaviors and efforts. When you reward yourself for your hard work and dedication, you are more inclined to continue those efforts in the future.

REDUCES STRESS

Taking time to celebrate achievements can reduce stress and increase feelings of happiness and contentment. It provides a break from the daily grind and allows you to enjoy the fruits of your labor.

ACKNOWLEDGES PROGRESS

Celebrating achievements allows you to acknowledge how far you've come. It's a reminder of your progress and the steps you've taken to reach your goals.

INSPIRES OTHERS

Your celebrations can inspire and motivate others. When friends, family, or colleagues see you celebrating your achievements, it can encourage them to pursue their own goals and celebrate their successes.

DAY 5: THE POWER OF CELEBRATION

FOSTERS A POSITIVE MINDSET

Celebration reinforces a positive mindset. It helps you focus on the positive aspects of your life and accomplishments, which can improve your overall outlook on life.

STRENGTHENS RELATIONSHIPS

Sharing your achievements with others can strengthen your relationships. Celebrating together can create a sense of camaraderie and connection with friends, family, and colleagues.

BALANCES LIFE

Celebrating achievements can provide balance in your life. While it's important to set and pursue goals, it's equally important to take breaks and enjoy the fruits of your labor.

In conclusion, celebrating your achievements is not only a way to acknowledge your hard work and success but also a means to boost your confidence, motivation, and overall well-being. It's an important practice that can help you maintain a positive outlook on life and continue to pursue your goals and dreams with enthusiasm.

Felicia's Grace Gems

REFERENCE SCRIPTURE | COLOSSIANS 3:17 (NIV)
And whatever you do, whether in word or deed, do it all in the name of the Lord Jesus, giving thanks to God the Father through him.

PRAYER POINT | GRATITUDE AND POSITIVITY
Express gratitude for the positive aspects of your life.
Pray for a positive and hopeful outlook.

APPLICATION

Create a mood board filled with images, quotes, and symbols that represent mental wellness and self-care for women, inspiring them to visualize their own journey to well-being.

DAY 6: UGHHHHH.....SETBACKS

Learning from difficult experiences or setbacks as a Christian involves a combination of faith, self-reflection, and seeking guidance from biblical teachings. Here are some steps to help you navigate such situations:

SEEK BIBLICAL GUIDANCE

Look to the Bible for wisdom and guidance. Many biblical stories involve individuals facing setbacks and overcoming them with God's help. For example, the story of Job, who faced immense suffering, can provide insights into perseverance and faith in the face of adversity.

FORGIVENESS

If the setback involves someone else's actions, practice forgiveness. Remember that forgiveness is a central teaching in Christianity. It doesn't mean condoning the wrongdoing but letting go of bitterness and resentment.

LEARN AND GROW

Consider what lessons can be drawn from the experience. How can you grow spiritually and personally from this setback? This may involve recognizing areas where you need to improve or making changes in your life.

TRUST GOD'S PLAN

Remember that God works in mysterious ways, and setbacks may be part of His plan for your life. Trust that He has a purpose for everything, even if it's not immediately clear.

STAY POSITIVE

Maintain a positive attitude. It's easy to become discouraged during difficult times, but remember that God is with you, and your faith can provide you with the strength to persevere.

DAY 6: UGHHHHH.....SETBACKS

PROFESSIONAL HELP

Sometimes, a difficult experience may be too overwhelming to navigate on your own. Don't hesitate to seek professional counseling or therapy if needed. God provides resources, including mental health professionals, to help you heal and grow.

CONTINUE IN FAITH

Remember that setbacks are a part of life, but your faith can help you navigate them. Keep your faith strong, continue to study the Bible, and stay connected to your Christian community.

In summary, learning from difficult experiences or setbacks as a Christian involves relying on your faith, seeking guidance from the Bible, and using the support of your church community to grow spiritually and personally through challenging times. Trust in God's plan, practice forgiveness, and maintain a positive attitude as you navigate these experiences.

Felicia's Grace Gems

REFERENCE SCRIPTURE | JAMES 1:2-4 (NIV)

Consider it pure joy, my brothers and sisters, whenever you face trials of many kinds, because you know that the testing of your faith produces perseverance. Let perseverance finish its work so that you may be mature and complete, not lacking anything.

PRAYER POINT | CLARITY AND WISDOM

Ask for clarity of mind and wisdom to make sound decisions and navigate difficult situations.

APPLICATION

Explore a life lesson you've learned from a difficult experience or setback.

Emotional Wellness

Hey Sis Hey,

Emotional wellness is like a compass that guides us through life. Our emotions play a vital role in our everyday functioning, mood and overall well-being. It is critical that we are in tune with our emotions as it impacts our overall quality of life. It is important to embrace, understand, and manage our emotions in healthy ways.

Being emotionally whole, allows you to cultivate inner peace and resilience. When you are emotionally strong you are not easily moved when life throws you blows. With the ups, downs, and uncertainty of life, we have the internal strength and capacity to navigate storms.

The various roles women have in life can sometimes wear on their emotions due to the demands and expectations. A quick solution is effective time management and setting boundaries. Prioritize self-care, delegate tasks when possible, and communicate openly with loved ones to manage these roles more effectively and reduce emotional strain.

One key aspect of balance is the ability to delegate effectively. Personally, I find this challenging because I have a strong desire to maintain control (all the time) and ensure everything is executed perfectly. Delegating tasks and not attempting to handle everything myself is an ongoing struggle. It' s crucial for us to delegate tasks that become overwhelming or that others are fully capable of handling. Equally important is the ability to say 'no' when necessary, and not guilting yourself about it. Creating boundaries and inserting peace of mind. Whether you know it or not, being emotionally well enhances our relationships. When we understand and manage our emotions, we can communicate more effectively, empathize with others, and build deeper, more meaningful connections. True freedom.

By gaining insight into your thoughts and inner self, you give yourself the opportunity to understand what truly matters in your life, your personal growth and self-awareness.

When you prioritize your emotional wellness, you not only enhance your quality of life but also embark on a spiritual exploration of self-discovery and growth. Embrace your emotions as a source of wisdom and let it guide you towards a more meaningful and spiritually enriched existence.

Gracefully Submitted,

" Your sparkle defines your essence; never let it fade away."

-F.E.W

DAY 7: IT'S TIME FOR SELF-CARE!

Having a self-care ritual as a Christian is important for several reasons:

PHYSICAL WELL-BEING

The Bible teaches that our bodies are temples of the Holy Spirit (1 Corinthians 6:19-20). Taking care of your physical health through self-care rituals, such as exercise, proper nutrition, and rest, is a way to honor this teaching.

MENTAL AND EMOTIONAL WELL-BEING

Self-care can help you manage stress, anxiety, and negative emotions. It allows you to maintain a healthy mind and emotional balance, which is essential for living out your faith effectively.

SPIRITUAL GROWTH

Self-care rituals can create space for spiritual growth and reflection. Regular prayer, meditation, and reading of scripture can be part of your self-care routine, helping you connect with God on a deeper level.

SERVICE TO OTHERS

Christians are called to love and serve others. However, you cannot pour from an empty cup. Self-care ensures that you are emotionally and physically well-equipped to serve others with love and compassion.

SETTING BOUNDARIES

Self-care rituals can help you establish healthy boundaries in your life. This prevents burnout and allows you to prioritize what truly matters, including your relationship with God and your family.

STRENGTHENING FAITH

Spending time in prayer, meditation, and Bible study as part of your self-care can strengthen your faith. It provides an opportunity to seek God's guidance, gain wisdom, and deepen your understanding of His Word.

DAY 7: IT'S TIME FOR SELF-CARE!

ENHANCING RELATIONSHIPS

Taking care of yourself can improve your relationships with others. When you are emotionally and mentally well, you are better able to engage in meaningful, positive relationships with family, friends, and fellow believers.

SETTING AN EXAMPLE

By practicing self-care as a Christian, you set an example for others, including your family and fellow believers. Your commitment to self-care can inspire and encourage others to prioritize their well-being as well.

In summary, self-care rituals are essential for Christians because they promote physical, mental, emotional, and spiritual well-being. They enable you to live out your faith more effectively, serve others, and honor the teachings of the Bible regarding the care of your body and mind.

Felicia's Grace Gems

REFERENCE SCRIPTURE | MARK 6:31 (NIV)
Then, because so many people were coming and going that they did not even have a chance to eat, he said to them, 'Come with me by yourselves to a quiet place and get some rest.

PRAYER POINT | AWARENESS
Pray for self-awareness to recognize when you need self-care and what specific practices would benefit you most.

PRAYER POINT | PRIORITIZATION
Ask God to help you prioritize self-care as an essential part of maintaining your health and well-being.

APPLICATION

Describe a self-care ritual that always leaves you feeling refreshed and rejuvenated.

DAY 8: PERSONAL GROWTH AND RESILIENCE

Personal growth and resilience are important aspects of a Christian's life, encompassing spiritual, emotional, and practical development in the face of challenges.

Here's a closer look at Personal Growth:

CHARACTER DEVELOPMENT

Personal growth involves developing Christ-like character traits, often referred to as the fruit of the Spirit (Galatians 5:22-23). These include love, joy, peace, patience, kindness, goodness, faithfulness, gentleness, and self-control.

KNOWLEDGE AND WISDOM

Christians seek to grow in their understanding of God's Word and the principles of their faith. This involves gaining knowledge and wisdom to apply biblical teachings to daily life.

SERVICE AND MINISTRY

Personal growth includes discovering and using your spiritual gifts for service and ministry within the church and the community. It's about finding your purpose and fulfilling it in line with God's plan for your life.

FORGIVENESS AND GRACE

Growing as a Christian also involves learning to forgive others as Christ has forgiven us and extending grace to those who may have wronged us.

Here's a closer look at Resilience:

FAITH-BASED RESILIENCE

Christian resilience is rooted in faith. It means trusting in God's sovereignty and His plan even in the face of adversity. It involves believing that God is with you and will provide the strength to endure challenges.

DAY 8: PERSONAL GROWTH AND RESILIENCE

PERSEVERANCE

Resilience means enduring through trials and tribulations with patience and perseverance, knowing that they can lead to spiritual growth and maturity (James 1:2-4).

HOPE

Christian resilience is anchored in hope, the confident expectation of God's promises. This hope can sustain you during tough times, reminding you that God is working all things together for good (Romans 8:28).

RESTORATION

In Christian resilience, there is room for restoration and healing. This may involve seeking reconciliation, seeking professional help when needed, and allowing God's grace to bring wholeness.

In summary, personal growth as a Christian encompasses spiritual, character, and service development, while resilience is rooted in faith, hope, and perseverance, with a reliance on God's guidance and the support of a Christian community. Both personal growth and resilience are essential for navigating life's challenges while growing in your relationship with God.

Felicia's Grace Gems

REFERENCE SCRIPTURE| ROMANS 12:2 (NIV)
Do not conform to the pattern of this world, but be transformed by the renewing of your mind. Then you will be able to test and approve what God's will is—his good, pleasing and perfect will.

PRAYER POINT | WISDOM
Ask for wisdom and discernment to make wise choices and decisions that contribute to your personal growth.

APPLICATION

Write about a challenging moment in your life that ultimately led to personal growth and resilience.

DAY 9: SELF-AFFIRMATION

Self-affirmation refers to the practice of consciously and positively recognizing and asserting one's own values, beliefs, abilities, and worth. It involves acknowledging your positive qualities and reinforcing your self-esteem and self-confidence. Self-affirmation can take various forms, including thoughts, statements, or actions that reinforce a positive self-image.

Here are some key aspects of self-affirmation:

POSITIVE STATEMENTS

Self-affirmation often involves making positive statements about yourself. These statements can focus on your strengths, achievements, and values. For example, you might say, "I am capable of overcoming challenges" or "I am a loving and compassionate person."

COUNTERACTING NEGATIVE THOUGHTS

Self-affirmation can help counteract negative self-talk and self-doubt. When faced with self-criticism or self-critical thoughts, you can use self-affirmations to challenge and replace these negative beliefs with more positive and constructive ones.

BUILDING SELF-CONFIDENCE

Regular self-affirmation can boost your self-confidence and self-esteem. It reminds you of your capabilities and worth, helping you approach challenges with a more positive and resilient mindset.

REDUCING STRESS AND ANXIETY

Engaging in self-affirmation can reduce stress and anxiety by promoting a sense of self-worth and self-acceptance. It can help you feel more in control and capable of handling life's challenges.

IMPROVING MENTAL HEALTH

Regular self-affirmation is associated with improved mental health outcomes. It can contribute to a more positive self-image and reduce symptoms of depression and anxiety.

DAY 9: SELF-AFFIRMATION

FOSTERING A GROWTH MINDSET

Self-affirmation aligns with the concept of a growth mindset, which is the belief that one can develop and improve through effort and learning. When you affirm your abilities and potential, you are more likely to embrace challenges as opportunities for growth.

ALIGNING WITH VALUES

Self-affirmation can help you align your actions and decisions with your core values and beliefs. It reminds you of what is most important to you and can guide your choices in life.

It's important to note that self-affirmation is not about being overly self-centered or denying areas where you need to improve. Instead, it is a practice that promotes a healthy sense of self-worth and self-acceptance, which can be valuable for personal growth, well-being, and achieving your goals.

Felicia's Grace Gems

REFERENCE SCRIPTURE | PSALM 139:13-14 (NIV)

For you created my inmost being; you knit me together in my mother's womb. I praise you because I am fearfully and wonderfully made; your works are wonderful, I know that full well.

PRAYER POINT | SELF-ACCEPTANCE

Pray for the ability to fully accept and embrace yourself as you are, recognizing your inherent worth and value.

PRAYER POINT | OVERCOMING INSECURITIES

Seek God's guidance in overcoming insecurities and self-doubt that may be holding you back.

APPLICATION

Describe your favorite self-affirmation and how it empowers you.
For Example: I am Loved! I am Accepted! I will prosper! I am Free!

Hey Sis Hey,

It is my goal in this letter is to convey the importance and benefits of nurturing your physical well-being. Your physical health serves as the foundation for your entire life, extending beyond looks or fitness. It is a way to honor and recognize the spiritual value of your body. Prioritizing your physical well-being brings forth numerous rewards.

To nurture your physical health, make regular exercise, a balanced diet, and sufficient rest a priority. Listen to your body' s needs and heed to its signals. Explore physical activities that resonate with your soul and bring joy to your heart. Remember, caring for your physical health is not self-centered but rather an essential step on your spiritual path. It empowers you to effectively serve others and the world.

If you do not know where to start, seek help from health professionals, and communities that share your wellness goals.

As women get older, important medical exams and screenings may include:

- Mammograms: Regular breast cancer screenings, typically starting at age 40 or as recommended by a healthcare provider.
- Pap Smears: Regular cervical cancer screenings, usually starting at age 21 and continuing at intervals recommended by a healthcare provider.
- Bone Density Test: Screening for osteoporosis, often recommended starting around menopause or as advised by a doctor.
- Cholesterol Test: Monitoring cholesterol levels, especially if there is a family history of heart disease or other risk factors.
- Blood Pressure Check: Regular blood pressure monitoring to assess cardiovascular health.
- Colonoscopy: Screening for colorectal cancer, typically recommended starting at age 50 or earlier if there are risk factors.
- Mammogram: Bone density testing, which may start around menopause to assess bone health.

It's important for women to consult with their healthcare providers to determine the appropriate timing and frequency of these exams based on individual health history and risk factors.

Together, we can inspire and support one another on our journey towards a more vibrant, spiritually enriched life. May you embrace the sacredness of your physical being and discover the significance in maintaining your physical wellness.

Gracefully submitted,

Felicia Willis

She was a captivating blend of beauty and strength, igniting the cosmos.

———

- F . E . W

DAY 10: THE CONNECTION

Regular exercise and a healthy lifestyle have a profoundly positive impact on your overall quality of life. Here are some of the key ways in which they contribute to an improved quality of life:

PHYSICAL HEALTH

- Exercise helps maintain a healthy weight and reduces the risk of obesity-related conditions like heart disease, diabetes, and certain cancers.
- It strengthens the cardiovascular system, improves blood circulation, and lowers blood pressure.
- Regular physical activity supports the health of bones and muscles, reducing the risk of osteoporosis and improving overall mobility.

MENTAL HEALTH

- Exercise is known to reduce symptoms of depression and anxiety. It promotes the release of endorphins, which are natural mood lifters.
- It enhances cognitive function and memory, reducing the risk of age-related cognitive decline.
- Physical activity can help manage stress and improve sleep quality, which are crucial for mental well-being.

ENERGY AND VITALITY

- Regular exercise increases energy levels and reduces fatigue, allowing you to engage more fully in daily activities.
- It promotes better sleep, helping you wake up feeling refreshed and energized.

SOCIAL AND EMOTIONAL WELL-BEING

- Engaging in group fitness activities or sports can foster social connections and a sense of community.
- Exercise provides an opportunity for relaxation and "me time," allowing you to de-stress and rejuvenate emotionally.

DAY 10: THE CONNECTION

PRODUCTIVITY AND FOCUS

- Regular physical activity is linked to increased productivity and better concentration, both at work and in daily life.
- It helps with time management and mental clarity.

QUALITY OF RELATIONSHIPS

- A healthy lifestyle can positively affect your relationships by promoting well-being and reducing mood swings and irritability.
- Sharing fitness activities with a partner or friends can strengthen social bonds.

QUALITY OF SLEEP

- Regular exercise can improve sleep patterns and reduce the occurrence of sleep disorders like insomnia.

Incorporating regular exercise and adopting a healthy lifestyle is a holistic approach to enhancing your quality of life. It not only benefits your physical health but also has profound positive effects on your mental, emotional, and social well-being. It empowers you to lead a fuller, more vibrant life with increased longevity and an improved sense of overall well-being.

Felicia's Grace Gems

REFERENCE SCRIPTURE | 1 CORINTHIANS 6:19-20 (NIV)

Do you not know that your bodies are temples of the Holy Spirit, who is in you, whom you have received from God? You are not your own; you were bought at a price. Therefore honor God with your bodies.

PRAYER POINT | STRENGTH

Ask for physical strength to maintain a healthy body and mental strength to face life's challenges.

APPLICATION

Consider the connection between your physical and mental wellness. How does regular exercise and a healthy lifestyle positively affect your overall quality of life.

DAY 11: PERSONAL STRENGTHS

Discovering your personal strengths as a woman is a valuable process that can help you build self-confidence, pursue your passions, and achieve your goals. Here are some steps to help you uncover and embrace your personal strengths:

SELF-REFLECTION

- Take time for introspection. Reflect on your life experiences, accomplishments, and challenges. Think about moments when you felt most confident and empowered.
- Consider your interests, hobbies, and activities that you enjoy. What activities make you feel most alive and engaged? These can provide clues about your strengths.

PERSONALITY ASSESSMENTS

- Consider taking personality assessments like the Myers-Briggs Type Indicator (MBTI), StrengthsFinder, or the Enneagram. These assessments can provide insights into your personality traits and strengths.
- While these assessments are not definitive, they can offer valuable insights into your preferences and tendencies.

JOURNALING

- Keep a journal to record your thoughts, feelings, and experiences. Write about moments when you felt most confident, accomplished, or in your element.
- Reviewing your journal over time may reveal patterns that point to your strengths.

MENTORSHIP AND COACHING

- Take time for introspection. Reflect on your life experiences, accomplishments, and challenges. Think about moments when you felt most confident and empowered.
- Consider your interests, hobbies, and activities that you enjoy. What activities make you feel most alive and engaged? These can provide clues about your strengths.

DAY 11: PERSONAL STRENGTHS

EXPERIMENT AND TAKE RISKS

- Be willing to step out of your comfort zone and try new things. Taking on challenges and risks can help you discover hidden strengths.
- Don't be afraid to fail or make mistakes; these experiences can be valuable in uncovering strengths.

PASSIONS AND VALUES

- Consider what matters most to you and what you are passionate about. Your values and passions often align with your strengths because they are what drive you.
- Think about how you can use your strengths to further your passions and values.

CELEBRATE YOUR ACHIEVEMENTS

- Acknowledge and celebrate your accomplishments, no matter how small they may seem. Recognizing your achievements can boost your self-esteem and reveal your strengths.

Remember that discovering your personal strengths is an ongoing process. Your strengths may evolve over time, and it's essential to embrace them and use them to pursue your goals and make a positive impact on the world.

Felicia's Grace Gems

REFERENCE SCRIPTURE | 1 CORINTHIANS 12:4-6 (NIV)

There are different kinds of gifts, but the same Spirit distributes them. There are different kinds of service, but the same Lord. There are different kinds of working, but in all of them and in everyone it is the same God at work.

PRAYER POINT | ALIGNMENT WITH VALUES

Ask God to help you use your strengths in ways that align with your values and principles. Pray for wisdom in making choices that honor your beliefs.

APPLICATION

What are your top three personal strengths, and how do they contribute to your self-esteem?

DAY 12: FUNDAMENTALS OF PHYSICAL WELLNESS

Physical wellness is a fundamental aspect of overall well-being and involves taking care of your body to promote good health and prevent illness or injury. Here are the fundamentals of physical wellness:

REGULAR EXERCISE

- Engage in regular physical activity, which can include aerobic exercises (like walking, jogging, or swimming), strength training, flexibility exercises, and balance training.
- Aim for at least 150 minutes of moderate-intensity aerobic exercise or 75 minutes of vigorous-intensity aerobic exercise per week, as recommended by the World Health Organization.

BALANCED DIET

- Maintain a balanced diet that includes a variety of fruits, vegetables, whole grains, lean proteins, and healthy fats.
- Limit or avoid excessive consumption of sugary, processed, and high-fat foods.
- Stay hydrated by drinking plenty of water throughout the day.

ADEQUATE SLEEP

- Prioritize getting enough sleep each night, typically 7-9 hours for adults. Quality sleep is crucial for physical and mental well-being.
- Establish a consistent sleep schedule and create a relaxing bedtime routine.

HYGIENE AND PERSONAL CARE

- Practice good personal hygiene, including regular bathing, dental care, and grooming.
- Maintain a skincare routine to protect your skin from the sun and other environmental factors.

STRESS MANAGEMENT

- Practice stress-reduction techniques, such as mindfulness, meditation, deep breathing exercises, or yoga.
- Manage your workload and responsibilities to reduce chronic stress..

DAY 12: FUNDAMENTALS OF PHYSICAL WELLNESS

HEALTHY RELATIONSHIPS

- Cultivate healthy relationships that provide emotional support and a sense of belonging.
- Seek help or counseling when facing relationship issues or domestic violence.

PHYSICAL REST AND RECOVERY

- Practice good personal hygiene, including regular bathing, dental care, and grooming.
- Maintain a skincare routine to protect your skin from the sun and other environmental factors.

CONSISTENT HYDRATION

- Maintain proper hydration by drinking water throughout the day. Adequate hydration supports various bodily functions and helps prevent dehydration.

Physical wellness is an ongoing journey that involves making healthy choices and maintaining positive habits. By prioritizing physical wellness, you can enhance your overall quality of life, increase your longevity, and enjoy a greater sense of vitality and well-being.

Felicia's Grace Gems

REFERENCE SCRIPTURE | 1 TIMOTHY 4:8 (NIV)

For physical training is of some value, but godliness has value for all things, holding promise for both the present life and the life to come.

PRAYER POINT | SELF-CONTROL

Pray for self-control and discipline to make choices that benefit your physical health. Ask God to help you resist unhealthy temptations and develop good habits.

APPLICATION

If you were to design a wellness challenge for yourself, what activities and goals would you set to promote physical wellness? How would you assess the success and challenges?

Hey Sis Hey,

I want to take a moment to emphasize the importance of our social wellness journey.

And need for positive interactions with others. Our connections with others, the bonds we nurture, and the impact we have on our various communities are all integral parts of our social well-being. As we navigate our path towards social wellness, my hope is that we find meaningful connections that bring joy, support, and a sense of belonging. May our relationships be a source of strength during difficult times and a bridge for shared laughter and cherished memories.

The COVID-19 pandemic drastically altered the dynamics of social engagement worldwide. It brought about heightened social apprehension as people battled with the fear of infection vs social engagement. Social distancing measures, lockdowns, and mask mandates became the norm, leading to reduce in-person interactions and an increase in virtual communication. These changes altered our traditional methods and forced individuals to adapt to a new way of connecting with others. As we break free of those fears and assimilate back into our traditional social functioning, I challenge you to take steps towards engagement and making deliberate attempts to recognize fears and defeat apprehensiveness.

In this journey, we have the opportunity to inspire and uplift those around us, creating a positive ripple effect in our community. Your actions, kindness, and empathy can make a significant difference in the lives of others.

Dealing with the fear of fitting in and embracing your true self, requires us to delve deep into our self-conception. Before we can share our authentic self with the world we have to truly understand and explore our insecurities.

Acceptance and fitting in should never come at the cost of sacrificing your authenticity. Guard yourself against mistreatment by others and maintain a sense of harmony in your life by not allowing every situation to disrupt it. Embrace who you are, explore your insecurities, and share your true self with the world, while staying true to your values and beliefs.

Remember, your social wellness is a reflection of your beautiful spirit. Embrace it, nurture it, and let it be a testament to the incredible impact you can have on the world.

Gracefully submitted,

Felicia Willis

Embrace

THE CHALLENGE OF SHINING BRIGHTLY AND IGNITING YOUR INNER FIRE.

— F.E.W

DAY 13: #GOALS

Finding a role model as a Christian woman can be a valuable and inspiring endeavor. Role models can help guide your spiritual journey, provide encouragement, and offer examples of how to live out your faith. Here are some steps to help you find a Christian role model:

PRAYER AND SEEKING GUIDANCE

- Begin by seeking guidance through prayer. Ask God to lead you to the right role model or mentor who can inspire and guide you in your faith journey.
- Pray for wisdom and discernment to recognize the right person when you encounter them.

CHURCH COMMUNITY

- Your church community is an excellent place to find potential role models. Attend church services, small group meetings, and events to connect with fellow believers who may serve as role models.
- Look for individuals who exhibit strong faith, wisdom, and a Christ-like character within your church.

MENTORSHIP PROGRAMS

- Many churches and Christian organizations offer mentorship programs specifically designed to pair individuals with mentors or role models.
- Inquire if your church or a Christian organization in your area has such a program.

BOOKS AND MEDIA

- Keep a journal to record your thoughts, feelings, and experiences. Write about moments when you felt most confident, accomplished, or in your element.
- Reviewing your journal over time may reveal patterns that point to your strengths.

DAY 13: #GOALS

ONLINE COMMUNITIES

- Explore online Christian communities, forums, and social media groups where Christian women share their faith journeys, testimonies, and provide support.
- Engage in discussions and connect with individuals whose stories resonate with you.

PERSONAL INTERACTIONS

- Pay attention to the Christian women in your life who exhibit qualities and values you admire. This could be a family member, friend, or colleague.
- Initiate conversations and build relationships with these women to learn from their experiences.

When you find a potential role model, it's essential to approach the relationship with humility and a willingness to learn. Remember that no one is perfect, and even role models have their flaws. Consider how their journey aligns with your own faith and values, and be open to the guidance and wisdom they can offer as you navigate your own Christian walk.

Felicia's Grace Gems

REFERENCE SCRIPTURE | HEBREWS 13:7 (NIV)

Remember your leaders, who spoke the word of God to you. Consider the outcome of their way of life and imitate their faith.

PRAYER POINT | GOD'S GUIDANCE

Seek God's guidance in the process of finding a role model. Pray for His wisdom to lead you to the right person who aligns with your values and goals.

APPLICATION

Write about a role model or woman who inspires you and the qualities you admire in her.

DAY 14: THE AUDACITY

Challenging relationships or friendships can be a part of life for anyone, including Christian women. Navigating these difficulties while maintaining your Christian values and principles can be challenging, but it's possible. Here are some tips for handling challenging relationships or friendships as a Christian woman:

PRAYER AND REFLECTION

- Start by seeking God's guidance through prayer. Ask for wisdom, patience, and discernment to understand the situation and your role in it.
- Reflect on your own feelings, actions, and attitudes within the relationship. Consider whether there are areas where you can improve.

FORGIVENESS AND GRACE

- As a Christian, forgiveness is central to your faith. Practice forgiveness even when it's difficult. Remember that forgiveness does not necessarily mean reconciliation but releasing bitterness and resentment.
- Extend grace to the other person as God has extended grace to you.

FOCUS ON SELF-IMPROVEMENT

- Establish healthy boundaries in the relationship. Clearly communicate your boundaries and expectations and respect theirs as well.
- Boundaries help maintain a sense of balance and respect in the relationship.

KNOW WHEN TO LET GO:

- Sometimes, despite your efforts, a relationship may remain toxic or harmful. In such cases, it may be necessary to distance yourself or even end the relationship for your well-being and safety.
- Seek guidance from a trusted spiritual advisor if you are uncertain about whether to maintain or end the relationship.

DAY 14: THE AUDACITY

Remember that every relationship is unique, and there is no one-size-fits-all solution to handling challenging relationships or friendships. Your faith and reliance on God's guidance can be your source of strength as you navigate these challenges. Keep in mind the biblical principles of love, forgiveness, and grace as you work towards resolution and growth in your relationships.

Felicia's Grace Gems

REFERENCE SCRIPTURE | COLOSSIANS 3:13 (NIV)

Bear with each other and forgive one another if any of you has a grievance against someone. Forgive as the Lord forgave you.

PRAYER POINT | PATIENCE AND UNDERSTANDING

Pray for patience and understanding to see the situation from the other person's perspective. Ask God to help you empathize with their feelings and experiences.

PRAYER POINT | TRANSFORMATION

Pray for transformation within the relationship, that both you and the other person may grow, learn, and become better individuals as a result.

APPLICATION

Reflect on a challenging relationship or friendship. What lessons have you learned from it? Where do you go from there?

DAY 15: EXPRESSING GRATITUDE

Expressing gratitude to someone who has had a significant positive influence on your life is a meaningful and important gesture. Here are some steps to help you thank that person in a thoughtful and heartfelt way:

CHOOSE THE RIGHT MOMENT

Find an appropriate time and place to express your gratitude. It could be in person, through a letter or email, or even during a special occasion like a birthday or anniversary.

BE SINCERE AND SPECIFIC

Be sincere in your gratitude and specific about how the person has influenced your life. Mention specific actions, qualities, or advice that have made a difference to you.

USE CLEAR AND EXPRESSIVE LANGUAGE

Use clear and expressive language to convey your feelings. Avoid overly formal or generic expressions of thanks. Be genuine and heartfelt in your words.

START WITH A WARM GREETING

Begin your message with a warm greeting, addressing the person by name. Express your appreciation right from the start.

EXPRESS YOUR GRATITUDE

Clearly state that you are grateful for their positive influence in your life. Use phrases like:
- "I wanted to express my deep gratitude for..."
- "I'm so thankful for the impact you've had on my life..."
- "Your kindness and support have meant the world to me..."

SHARE SPECIFIC EXAMPLES

Share specific examples of how their influence has made a difference. For instance:
- "Your guidance and mentorship helped me navigate a challenging time in my career."
- "Your friendship and encouragement during my health crisis gave me the strength to keep going."

DAY 15: EXPRESSING GRATITUDE

ACKNOWLEDGE THEIR QUALITIES

Acknowledge the person's qualities or characteristics that you admire and appreciate. For example:
- "Your unwavering faith, kindness, and generosity inspire me every day."
- "Your patience, wisdom, and selflessness have been a true blessing in my life."

EXPRESS THE IMPACT

Describe how their influence has impacted your life, whether it's personal growth, achieving goals, or finding happiness:
- "Because of you, I've grown as a person and achieved things I never thought possible."
- "Your positivity and encouragement have brought so much joy into my life."

CONCLUDE WITH GRATITUDE

End your message by expressing gratitude again and reiterating how much their influence means to you. Use phrases like:
- "I can't thank you enough for all you've done."
- "I am truly blessed to have you in my life."
- "Thank you from the bottom of my heart."

OFFER YOUR FUTURE SUPPORT

Let them know that you are there for them as well and that you are ready to support them if they ever need it.

PERSONALIZE THE MESSAGE

Tailor your thank-you message to your unique relationship with the person. Make it personal and genuine.

DAY 15: EXPRESSING GRATITUDE

FOLLOW UP

If possible, follow up your message with a small token of appreciation, such as a handwritten note, a thoughtful gift, or a kind gesture to show your gratitude in action.

Remember that expressing gratitude is a wonderful way to strengthen your bond with someone who has positively influenced your life. Your heartfelt words will likely mean a great deal to them and reinforce the positive impact they have had on you.

Felicia's Grace Gems

REFERENCE SCRIPTURE | COLOSSIANS 3:15 (NIV)

For we are God's handiwork, created in Christ Jesus to do good works, which God prepared in advance for us to do.

PRAYER POINT | IMPACT

Pray that your words have a positive impact on this person, reminding them of the significance of their influence and inspiring them to continue making a difference in others' lives.

PRAYER POINT | HUMILITY

Pray for humility in acknowledging the role this person has played in your life. Recognize that your gratitude is a reflection of God's grace through them.

APPLICATION

Send a gratitude letter to someone who has had a significant positive influence on your life.

Financial Wellness

Hey Sis Hey,

II hope this message finds you well. I wanted to take a moment to emphasize the importance of your financial wellness. Just as we nurture our physical and emotional health, it' s vital to care for our financial well-being.

Consider setting clear financial goals, budget wisely, and save for the future. Building a strong financial foundation will empower you to live life on your terms, pursue your dreams, and weather unexpected challenges. I'd like to stress the significance of your financial wellness and its broader impact, including spiritual benefits.

Being a good steward of your money not only ensures a secure future but also brings a sense of spiritual fulfillment. By managing your finances wisely, you can align your values with your financial choices, enabling you to live with greater purpose and intention.

Remember, financial wellness is not just about money; it's about gaining control, reducing stress, and achieving peace of mind. May your path to financial wellness be guided by both practical wisdom and the spiritual rewards that come from being a responsible steward of your resources.

Lastly, as a community, we need to consider the value of ensuring a stable future as a meaningful way to provide for your family down the road. Consulting with a financial advisor for wise investments, creating a comprehensive plan, and considering options such as trusts and life insurance to boost the inheritance you leave behind are all smart steps. Your thoughtful planning will leave a lasting impact on your loved ones. Too many times we rely on funding efforts like GoFundMe and other online petitions in place of financial responsibility and accountability.

Gracefully submitted,

Felicia Willis

Discover your unique brilliance, welcome it, and let it lead you towards success.

-F.E.W

DAY 16: CORE FINANCIAL VALUES

Core financial values are the fundamental principles and beliefs that guide an individual's or a family's approach to managing money and making financial decisions. These values serve as a foundation for financial behavior, helping individuals prioritize their financial goals and make ethical choices about money. Core financial values can vary from person to person but often include principles such as:

FINANCIAL RESPONSIBILITY

Taking responsibility for one's financial well-being by making informed decisions, setting financial goals, and budgeting responsibly. This value encourages individuals to avoid excessive debt and live within their means.

DEBT MANAGEMENT

Managing debt wisely, including paying off high-interest debt, avoiding unnecessary debt, and using credit responsibly. This value emphasizes the importance of not becoming burdened by debt.

FRUGALITY AND SIMPLICITY

Embracing a simple and frugal lifestyle that prioritizes needs over wants. This value encourages conscious spending and avoiding unnecessary expenses.

ETHICAL AND HONEST FINANCIAL PRACTICES

Conducting financial affairs with honesty, integrity, and ethical behavior. This includes paying bills on time, honoring financial commitments, and avoiding unethical financial practices.

LEGACY AND INHERITANCE

Planning for the transfer of wealth and assets to future generations, including estate planning and leaving a positive financial legacy.

DAY 16: CORE FINANCIAL VALUES

FINANCIAL INDEPENDENCE

Striving for financial independence and self-sufficiency, allowing individuals to make choices that align with their values and goals without financial constraints.

ENVIRONMENTAL AND SOCIAL RESPONSIBILITY

Considering the environmental and social impact of financial decisions, such as supporting sustainable and socially responsible investments and practices.

GENEROSITY AND GIVING

Recognizing the importance of giving back to the community and supporting charitable causes. This value emphasizes the joy of sharing financial blessings with others.

Core financial values can vary greatly among individuals and families, reflecting personal beliefs, cultural influences, and life experiences. It's essential to identify and prioritize your own core financial values to guide your financial decisions and align your money-related actions with your broader life goals and principles.

Felicia's Grace Gems

REFERENCE SCRIPTURE | 1 CORINTHIANS 16:2 (NIV)

On the first day of every week, each one of you should set aside a sum of money in keeping with your income, saving it up, so that when I come no collections will have to be made.

PRAYER POINT | DEBT FREEDOM

If applicable, pray for guidance and discipline in working toward debt freedom. Ask God for strength to overcome financial challenges.

PRAYER POINT | ALIGNMENT WITH GOD'S WILL

Seek to align your financial values with God's will and biblical principles. Pray for the strength to make choices that honor Him.

APPLICATION

What are your core financial values, and how do they guide your decisions and actions? For example, retirement, college fund, investment, etc.

DAY 17: WHAT'S IN YOUR EMERGENCY FUND?

An emergency fund is a financial safety net that consists of a dedicated savings account set aside for unexpected expenses or financial emergencies. It plays a crucial role in financial wellness by providing a buffer against unforeseen circumstances that could otherwise derail your financial stability and long-term goals. Here's why emergency funds are essential for financial well-being:

FINANCIAL PROTECTION

An emergency fund serves as a protective measure to cover unexpected expenses, such as medical bills, car repairs, home repairs, or job loss. Without one, you might be forced to rely on credit cards, loans, or deplete your other savings, which can lead to debt and financial stress.

REDUCES FINANCIAL STRESS

Knowing that you have an emergency fund in place can greatly reduce financial stress and anxiety. It provides peace of mind, knowing that you have a financial cushion to fall back on during challenging times.

PREVENTS DEBT ACCUMULATION

Having an emergency fund helps you avoid accumulating high-interest debt when unexpected expenses arise. Instead of relying on credit cards or loans, you can use your savings to cover the costs, saving you money in interest charges.

AVOIDS DIPPING INTO RETIREMENT SAVINGS

Some people dip into their retirement accounts to cover emergencies when they lack an emergency fund. This can have long-term financial consequences, including penalties and tax implications. An emergency fund protects your retirement savings.

ENABLES QUICK RESPONSE

Emergencies often require immediate action. With an emergency fund in place, you can respond quickly to situations like medical emergencies, home repairs, or unexpected job loss without having to scramble for funds.

DAY 17: WHAT'S YOUR EMERGENCY FUND?

PRESERVES CREDIT SCORE

Maintaining an emergency fund can help you avoid late payments or defaults on loans, which can negatively impact your credit score. A good credit score is essential for various financial opportunities, such as obtaining favorable loan terms.

To create and maintain a robust emergency fund, financial experts often recommend setting aside three to six months' worth of living expenses. However, the exact amount can vary based on your individual circumstances, including your job security, financial obligations, and risk tolerance. Building an emergency fund is typically done gradually by saving a portion of your income each month until you reach your desired goal.

In summary, an emergency fund is a vital component of financial wellness, providing financial security, peace of mind, and the ability to weather unexpected financial storms without jeopardizing your long-term financial goals.

Felicia's Grace Gems

REFERENCE SCRIPTURE | PROVERBS 21:20 (NIV)
The wise store up choice food and olive oil, but fools gulp
theirs down.

PRAYER POINT | FINANCIAL DISCIPLINE
Ask for strength and discipline to consistently contribute to
your emergency fund, even when faced with competing
financial demands.

APPLICATION

Discuss the concept of emergency funds' and their role in financial wellness. How much do you aim to save In your emergency fund, and what scenarios do you consider emergencies?

DAY 18: LET'S TALK MONEY!

Creating financial goals is an essential step in managing your finances effectively and working towards your desired financial future. Setting clear and achievable goals helps you stay focused, motivated, and accountable for your financial decisions. Here's a step-by-step guide to creating financial goals:

ASSESS YOUR CURRENT FINANCIAL SITUATION

Start by reviewing your current financial situation. This includes understanding your income, expenses, savings, debts, assets, and liabilities. Use budgeting tools or financial software to help you track your finances accurately.

DETERMINE YOUR SHORT-TERM AND LONG-TERM OBJECTIVES

Differentiate between short-term and long-term financial goals. Short-term goals are typically achievable within a year, while long-term goals may take several years to reach. Examples of short-term goals include paying off credit card debt, saving for a vacation, or building an emergency fund. Long-term goals may involve buying a home, saving for retirement, or funding your child's education.

BREAK DOWN LARGE GOALS INTO SMALLER MILESTONES

If you have significant long-term goals, break them down into smaller, manageable milestones. This makes the process less overwhelming and allows you to celebrate achievements along the way.

SET SPECIFIC DOLLAR AMOUNTS OR TARGETS

Assign specific dollar amounts or targets to your goals. Knowing how much you need to save or pay off makes it easier to track your progress.

STAY COMMITTED AND STAY MOTIVATED

Staying committed to your goals can be challenging, but remember why you set them in the first place. Visualize the benefits of achieving your goals to stay motivated.

DAY 18: LET'S TALK MONEY!

MAKE YOUR GOALS SPECIFIC, MEASURABLE, ACHIEVABLE, RELEVANT, AND TIME-BOUND (SMART)

- **Specific**: Clearly define what you want to achieve. For example, instead of saying, "I want to save money," specify, "I want to save $5,000 for a down payment on a house."
- **Measurable**: Set quantifiable criteria to track your progress. You should be able to measure your success and know when you've achieved your goal.
- **Achievable:** Ensure your goals are realistic and attainable within your financial means. Setting unattainable goals can lead to frustration and disappointment.
- **Relevant:** Align your goals with your values and priorities. Your financial goals should make sense within the context of your life.
- **Time-Bound:** Establish a deadline for achieving your goals. Having a timeline creates a sense of urgency and accountability.

Creating and pursuing financial goals is a continuous process that evolves as your life circumstances change. Regularly review and adjust your goals as needed to ensure they remain aligned with your financial aspirations and priorities.

Felicia's Grace Gems

REFERENCE SCRIPTURE | 1 TIMOTHY 6:10 (NIV)

For the love of money is a root of all kinds of evil. Some people, eager for money, have wandered from the faith and pierced themselves with many griefs.

PRAYER POINT | PROTECTION FROM TEMPTATIONS

Ask for protection from financial temptations and impulsive spending that can derail your goals.

APPLICATION

List 3 financial goals you would want to accomplish in the next year, and write a realistic budget that coincides with your goals.

Hey Sis Hey,

Let's jump right into it! Your intellectual well-being is a powerful force that shapes not only your understanding of the world but also your connection to the deeper spiritual dimensions of life. When you prioritize the cultivation of your mind, you begin a life changing movement with a load of rewards.

Intellectual wellness is not about intelligence but about the journey of seeking knowledge and wisdom. It's about staying open to new ideas and continuously expanding your understanding of the world and yourself.

I value transparency and would like to share how I feed my intellectual development needs. I enjoy becoming a member of new groups and organizations that help me stay up-to-date and act as a valuable source of fresh, innovative ideas and connections. I've been involved in motherhood collectives to expand my understanding as a parent, participated in PTO boards to gain insights into my kids as students, and enjoy attending leadership conferences to keep my mind agile and up to date with modern approaches to leadership and engaging people. Don't have the time or finances to commit? I spend time in social media groups on nutrition and learning about hazardous food products. There' s a group or organization out there perfectly suited for every facet of your identity.

Don't know exactly what you're interested in? Expand your reading horizons, delve into a variety of viewpoints, and participate in substantial discussions within your community. Look for mentors, teachers, and groups that promote intellectual development and nurture a sense of inquisitiveness.

Everyone's interests, perspectives, and viewpoints are unique. Do not be afraid to seek advice from those who inspire you. Collectively you can narrow down your interests and get involved in your next assignment on earth.

May your intellectual wellness be a beacon on your path to deeper spiritual insight and a source of boundless empowerment.

Gracefully submitted,

Felicia Willis

Life is too brief to hide
your luminosity.
Let it shine!

-F.E.W

DAY 19: WHAT'S YOUR HOBBY?

Having a hobby plays a significant role in enhancing your overall well-being and quality of life. Hobbies are activities or interests pursued for pleasure, relaxation, and personal enjoyment. Here are several reasons why having a hobby is important in your life:

STRESS REDUCTION

Hobbies provide an effective way to de-stress and relax. Engaging in activities you enjoy can help reduce the physical and mental effects of stress, such as tension and anxiety.

IMPROVED MENTAL HEALTH

Hobbies stimulate your mind and creativity. They can boost your mood, increase feelings of happiness, and reduce symptoms of depression and loneliness.

SENSE OF ACCOMPLISHMENT

Pursuing a hobby allows you to set and achieve goals, no matter how small. Accomplishing these goals can boost your self-esteem and self-confidence.

CREATIVITY AND INNOVATION

Hobbies often involve creativity and problem-solving. Engaging in creative activities can enhance your ability to think outside the box and apply creative thinking to other aspects of your life.

TIME MANAGEMENT

Hobbies encourage effective time management and help you balance your work, personal life, and leisure time more efficiently.

EMOTIONAL OUTLET

Hobbies can serve as an emotional outlet, allowing you to express your feelings and thoughts in a healthy and constructive way. This can be particularly helpful during challenging times.

DAY 19: WHAT'S YOUR HOBBY?

SENSE OF IDENTITY

Hobbies contribute to your sense of identity and self-expression. They are a way to explore your interests and passions, helping you better understand yourself.

ENJOYMENT AND FULFILLMENT

Ultimately, hobbies are about enjoying life and finding fulfillment in your leisure time. They offer a break from routine and give you something to look forward to.

PREVENTION OF BURNOUT

Engaging in a hobby can prevent burnout by providing a healthy outlet for stress and allowing you to recharge mentally and emotionally.

LEGACY AND TRADITIONS

Hobbies can be a way to pass down traditions, skills, and interests to future generations, creating lasting memories and connections.

Incorporating hobbies into your life is not just a luxury; it's a vital aspect of maintaining balance, happiness, and overall well-being. Finding and nurturing your hobbies can be a fulfilling and enjoyable part of your daily routine.

Felicia's Grace Gems

REFERENCE SCRIPTURE | EPHESIANS 2:10 NIV

For we are God's handiwork, created in Christ Jesus to do good works, which God prepared in advance for us to do.

PRAYER POINT | SPIRITUAL CONNECTION

Seek to connect with God through your hobbies. Ask Him to use your leisure activities as moments of reflection, meditation, or inspiration.

APPLICATION

Write about a hobby or activity that allows you to lose track of time and immerse yourself fully. If It takes more than 5 minutes to think of an answer, create one.

DAY 20: A TRIP TO THE FUTURE

Outlining your aspirations and hopes for the years ahead as a Christian woman is a powerful exercise that can help you align your goals with your faith and values. Here's a framework to help you articulate your aspirations and hopes:

SPIRITUAL GROWTH AND RELATIONSHIP WITH GOD

- Deepen your relationship with God through prayer, meditation, and regular Bible study.
- Strengthen your faith and trust in God's plan for your life.
- Seek spiritual mentors and communities that support your growth.
- Consider specific spiritual goals, such as participating in mission work or volunteering in your church.

FAMILY AND RELATIONSHIPS

- Nurture your relationships with your spouse, children, and extended family.
- Prioritize quality time with loved ones and build strong, God-centered bonds.
- Pray for your family's well-being and growth in faith.
- Foster a loving and supportive home environment that reflects Christian values.

CAREER AND PERSONAL GROWTH

- Set career goals that align with your values and skills.
- Seek opportunities for professional development and growth.
- Use your career as a platform to make a positive impact in your workplace and community.
- Balance your career ambitions with your family and spiritual life.

SERVICE AND GIVING

- Identify ways to serve and give back to your community and those in need.
- Volunteer your time and talents to charitable organizations and church initiatives.
- Practice generosity by tithing and supporting causes that resonate with your faith.

DAY 20: A TRIP TO THE FUTURE

HEALTH AND WELL-BEING

- Prioritize your physical health through regular exercise, a balanced diet, and adequate rest.
- Focus on mental and emotional well-being by managing stress and seeking professional help when needed.
- Practice self-care and mindfulness to maintain a healthy balance in your life.

PERSONAL VALUES AND CHARACTER DEVELOPMENT

- Continuously strive to embody Christian virtues such as love, kindness, patience, and humility.
- Set personal growth goals that align with your values and character development.
- Work on any areas of personal improvement and seek accountability from trusted friends or mentors.

IMPACT ON OTHERS

- Consider how you can positively impact the lives of others through your actions, words, and relationships.
- Aim to be a source of encouragement, support, and inspiration to those around you.
- Pray for discernment in identifying opportunities to make a difference in people's lives.

SETTING SPECIFIC GOALS AND MILESTONES

- Break down your aspirations into specific, achievable goals with clear timelines.
- Set both short-term and long-term milestones to track your progress.
- Regularly review and adjust your goals as you journey forward.

DAY 20: A TRIP TO THE FUTURE

TRUSTING GOD'S PLAN

- Maintain an attitude of trust and surrender to God's plan for your life, even when circumstances are uncertain.
- Pray for guidance and discernment in aligning your aspirations with God's will.

TRUSTING GOD'S PLAN

- Maintain an attitude of trust and surrender to God's plan for your life, even when circumstances are uncertain.
- Pray for guidance and discernment in aligning your aspirations with God's will.

Remember that your aspirations and hopes as a Christian woman are deeply personal and may evolve over time. Regularly revisit and update your goals and seek support and guidance from your faith community, mentors, and prayer as you work towards realizing your aspirations in the years ahead.

Felicia's Grace Gems

REFERENCE SCRIPTURE | PROVERBS 16:3 NIV
Commit to the LORD whatever you do, and he will establish your plans.

PRAYER POINT | COMMITMENT TO FAITH
Dedicate your future to God's faithfulness and care. Pray for a firm commitment to your faith as you journey ahead.

APPLICATION

Write a letter to your future self, outlining your aspirations and hopes for the years ahead.

DAY 21: MINDFULNESS 101

Mindfulness can play a valuable role in the life of a Christian by enhancing one's spiritual and personal growth, deepening their relationship with God, and promoting a sense of peace and presence. Here are some ways mindfulness can be integrated into the life of a Christian:

FOCUSED PRAYER AND MEDITATION

Mindfulness can help Christians focus their prayers and meditation on God. By being present in the moment, you can engage more deeply in prayer, listening to God, and experiencing His presence.

GRATITUDE AND THANKFULNESS

Mindfulness can cultivate an attitude of gratitude. Christians are encouraged to give thanks in all circumstances (1 Thessalonians 5:18), and mindfulness can help you recognize and appreciate the blessings in your life.

STRESS REDUCTION

Practicing mindfulness techniques such as deep breathing and meditation can help manage stress and anxiety, allowing you to maintain a sense of calm and trust in God's plan (Philippians 4:6-7).

SELF-REFLECTION AND SELF-EXAMINATION

Mindfulness provides an opportunity for self-reflection and self-examination, which can help Christians identify areas in their lives that may need repentance, growth, or alignment with God's will (Psalm 139:23-24).

COMPASSION AND EMPATHY

Mindfulness can cultivate empathy and compassion for others. It encourages Christians to love their neighbors as themselves (Mark 12:31) and to treat others with kindness and understanding.

DAY 21: MINDFULNESS 101

IMPROVED RELATIONSHIPS

By being fully present in your interactions with others, you can build stronger and more meaningful relationships, which is consistent with the Christian commandment to love one another (John 13:34-35).

DETOX FROM DISTRACTIONS

In a world filled with distractions, mindfulness can serve as a detox for the mind, allowing Christians to focus on what truly matters in their faith and relationship with God.

DISCERNMENT

Mindfulness can aid in discerning God's voice and guidance in daily life, helping Christians make decisions that align with His will (Proverbs 3:5-6).

It's important to note that mindfulness practices can take various forms, and not all may resonate with every Christian. Some may prefer traditional meditation techniques, while others may find mindfulness in everyday activities like walking, gardening, or journaling. The key is to approach mindfulness with a Christ-centered perspective, aligning it with your faith and using it as a tool to grow closer to God and live out your Christian values.

Felicia's Grace Gems

REFERENCE SCRIPTURE | COLOSSIANS 3:2 NIV
Set your minds on things above, not on earthly things.

PRAYER POINT | KNOWLEDGE
Pray for an open mind to eagerly explore new knowledge
and clarity in understanding complex concepts.

APPLICATION

What role does mindfulness play in your life? Describe your mindfulness practices. (Mindfulness: Present moment awareness, being fully aware of your thoughts, feelings, and body sensations)

Hey Sis Hey,

As women, we all love our coins, right? So, it's only right we dive into women in the workplace and our vocational wellness. Fearless women emerged as leaders and paved the way for greater gender equality and diversify, fostering a more inclusive and equitable professional landscape. How can we take that fuel and truly become active beneficiaries of the opportunities we hear about every day? I t starts with making a decision. A decision to CHOOSE YOU!

Your vocational wellness is not just about your job or career—it' s about aligning your work with your values, talents, and aspirations. When you prioritize vocational wellness, you open doors to a fulfilling life that extends beyond the confines of your workplace.

When you extend beyond the workplace, and enhance your skill sets, it enables you to live a life that aligns with God' s will and intention for your life.

Often times, women are juggling various roles, we neglect ourselves and our skill sets. Balancing multiple roles in life can be challenging for women, often leaving little time for skill development.

Maintaining balance in my roles as a wife, pastor' s wife (whew, Jesus), mom, business owner, and more can feel almost surreal. Some others may have to juggle school, work, and various life commitments. However, it' s a daily task that requires trial and error. Is everything perfect? No. Are there times when things get neglected? Yes. But we must learn to stumble and rise, to cry and become ' superwoman' once more, to scream and rejoin the game. Balancing life and its demands and doesn' t happen overnight; we are all a work in progress. So, what steps are you taking to ensure you' re on your way?

For me, it starts with creating a to-do list the night before. Does everything on the list get done? No, not always, but it helps me stay on track and manage my time more effectively.

Remember, my goal is not to force you to reach a specific status or job title, it' s about finding fulfillment and purpose in whatever you do. You're a GAME CHANGER!

Gracefully submitted,

Felicia Willis

THE RADIANCE
within you has the
POWER TO BRIGHTEN
even the darkest of corners

-F.E.W

DAY 22: IT'S THE BALANCE FOR ME

The concept of balance in life refers to achieving a harmonious equilibrium among various aspects of your life, ensuring that no single aspect dominates at the expense of others. Striking a balance involves allocating time, energy, and attention to different areas of your life, such as work, family, relationships, personal growth, health, and leisure, in a way that promotes overall well-being and satisfaction. Here are some key aspects of the concept of balance in your life:

WORK-LIFE BALANCE

Balancing your professional and personal life is essential to prevent burnout, maintain good mental and physical health, and nurture relationships with family and friends.

PHYSICAL AND MENTAL HEALTH

Balancing physical health through regular exercise, a balanced diet, and adequate rest, along with mental health through stress management and self-care, is crucial for overall well-being.

PERSONAL GROWTH

Balance involves setting aside time for personal development, self-improvement, and pursuing your passions and interests. This can include learning new skills, pursuing hobbies, or expanding your knowledge.

SPIRITUAL WELL-BEING

For many, a sense of balance includes spiritual growth and connection. This can involve engaging in religious or spiritual practices, meditation, or contemplation.

FLEXIBILITY AND ADAPTABILITY

Recognizing that life is dynamic and ever-changing, a balanced approach allows for flexibility and adaptability when circumstances evolve.

DAY 22: IT'S THE BALANCE FOR ME

REFLECTION AND GOAL SETTING

Regularly reflecting on your life and setting meaningful goals can help you maintain a sense of purpose and direction.

PRIORITIZATION

Learning to prioritize what truly matters to you and making conscious choices to align with your values is essential for achieving balance.

QUALITY OVER QUANTITY

Prioritizing the quality of your experiences and relationships over quantity can lead to a more fulfilling life.

Balancing these aspects may look different for each person and can evolve over time. What's essential is that your approach to balance aligns with your values and priorities and helps you lead a fulfilling, meaningful, and well-rounded life.

Felicia's Grace Gems

REFERENCE SCRIPTURE | ECCLESIASTES 3:1 NIV
There is a time for everything,
and a season for every activity under the heavens.

PRAYER POINT | SEEKING GOD'S WISDOM
Pray for God's wisdom and discernment to make wise decisions regarding your work commitments, priorities, and boundaries.

APPLICATION

Reflect on the concept of balance in your life. How do you maintain equilibrium between vocational and life balance?

DAY 23: IT'S ALL ABOUT THE JUGGLE

Achieving vocational balance, also known as work-life balance, is crucial for overall well-being and satisfaction in your career and personal life. Here are some strategies to help you achieve vocational balance:

SET CLEAR BOUNDARIES

- Establish clear boundaries between your work and personal life. Designate specific times for work and leisure activities.
- Avoid overworking or constantly checking work emails outside of work hours.

EFFECTIVE TIME MANAGEMENT

- Use time management techniques like to-do lists, calendars, and task prioritization to optimize your work hours.
- Make a schedule that includes dedicated time for relaxation, hobbies, and spending time with loved ones.

LEARN TO SAY NO

- Be selective about the commitments you take on at work and in your personal life. Don't overextend yourself.
- Saying "no" when necessary allows you to focus on what truly matters.

LEARN TO DISCONNECT

During your personal time, disconnect from work-related devices and technology to fully engage in leisure activities and spend quality time with loved ones.

Felicia's Grace Gems

REFERENCE SCRIPTURE | 2 PROVERBS 16:3 NIV
Commit to the Lord whatever you do,
and he will establish your plans.

PRAYER POINT | OPEN MINDSET
Pray for an open mind to eagerly explore new knowledge
and clarity in understanding complex concepts.

APPLICATION

Imagine you're mentoring someone on achieving vocational balance. Share your Insights, experiences and advice on how to find harmony.

DAY 24: OVERCOMING SELF-DOUBT

Overcoming self-doubt is a challenging but empowering journey that involves building confidence and self-belief. Here are some strategies to help you conquer self-doubt:

RECOGNIZE AND ACKNOWLEDGE SELF-DOUBT

The first step in overcoming self-doubt is to acknowledge its presence. Recognize when you're experiencing self-doubt and understand that it's a common human emotion.

CHALLENGE NEGATIVE SELF-TALK

Pay attention to the negative thoughts and self-criticisms that fuel self-doubt. Challenge these thoughts with evidence of your past successes and positive affirmations.

FOCUS ON YOUR STRENGTHS

Identify your strengths, talents, and accomplishments. Remind yourself of these qualities regularly to boost your self-esteem.

PRACTICE SELF-COMPASSION

Treat yourself with kindness and self-compassion. Remember that everyone faces self-doubt at times, and it's okay to be imperfect.

DEVELOP YOUR TALENTS AND SKILLS

Invest time in developing your talents and skills. When you gain competence in areas of interest, it can boost your self-confidence.

REMEMBER YOUR IDENTITY IN CHRIST

Understand and embrace your identity as a child of God. Recognize that your worth is not based on your achievements or the opinions of others but on your relationship with God.

DAY 24: OVERCOMING SELF-DOUBT

CHALLENGE NEGATIVE SELF-TALK

Pay attention to the negative thoughts and self-criticisms that fuel self-doubt. Challenge these thoughts with evidence of your past successes and positive affirmations.

FOCUS ON YOUR STRENGTHS

Identify your strengths, talents, and accomplishments. Remind yourself of these qualities regularly to boost your self-esteem.

PRACTICE SELF-COMPASSION

Treat yourself with kindness and self-compassion. Remember that everyone faces self-doubt at times, and it's okay to be imperfect.

Remember that overcoming self-doubt is a gradual process, and setbacks may occur. Be patient with yourself and continue practicing these strategies to build lasting confidence and self-assurance. It's a journey of self-discovery and personal growth that can lead to a more fulfilling and empowered life.

Felicia's Grace Gems

REFERENCE SCRIPTURE | 2 PROVERBS 16:3 NIV
Commit to the Lord whatever you do,
and he will establish your plans.

PRAYER POINT | CONFIDENCE IN GOD'S LOVE
Pray for a deep understanding of God's unconditional love
for you. Ask Him to help you internalize His love and
acceptance, which can counteract feelings of self-doubt.

PRAYER POINT | RELEASE FROM COMPARISONS
Pray for release from the trap of comparing yourself to
others. Ask God to help you find contentment and
confidence in who He created you to be.

APPLICATION

Write about a time when you overcame self-doubt and accomplished something you once thought impossible.

Hey Sis Hey,

This letter offers a playful twist to our usual conversations and is a little more lighthearted. I t reminds us that our lives and journey doesn't always have to delve into serious matters, and it's a chance to let our creative ideas flow freely. Who knew exploring creativity was a major part of your wellness. There is a large amount of creative energy that flows within you, whether you have tapped into it or not, IT IS THERE!

We can keep our creative spark alive by nurturing our passions, setting aside dedicated time for creativity, seeking inspiration from various sources, collaborating with like-minded individuals, and embracing a growth mindset that welcomes opportunities for creative growth. Additionally, taking breaks to recharge, practicing self-care, and exploring new experiences can help women stay creatively vibrant and inspired.

Don't know where to start? What groups or organizations are you a part of? Develop a starting point by addressing a specific need within a group or organization you belong to is crucial for several reasons. Firstly, it demonstrates proactive leadership and a commitment to the group' s success. Moreover, it provides a chance for you to apply your talents within a supportive environment among individuals who share similar values and a shared objective.

My creativity serves as the gateway through which I believe God opens doors of opportunity for me. Quick testimony, my husband had a vision for a year-round daycare in our church. While I had little interest and limited experience, I had confidence in my creativity and work ethic. I gathered a team and built a program that has since served hundreds of families. It started as a summer camp, and expanded into a full-time daycare, before and after-school program, led people to Christ, became an outreach ministry, and a major financial contributor to our church. This daycare is a staple in my community. This reminds me that one's yes and a spark of initiative can lead to unimaginable results.

Do not fear failure or judgment. Instead, embrace the joy of exploration and the thrill of experimentation. I leave you with this question, What life decision are you ONE "Yes" away from living? Tap into your creative juices and be bold enough to let it flow.

Gracefully submitted,

Felicia Willis

In a universe
abundant with stars,
choose to be the
supernova that
shines with utmost
intensity.

−F.E.W

DAY 25: EXPLORING CREATIVITY

Creativity plays a multifaceted and essential role in your life, influencing various aspects of your personal, professional, and overall well-being. Here are some key roles of creativity:

PROBLEM SOLVING

Creativity enables you to approach challenges and problems with fresh perspectives. It encourages you to think outside the box, identify innovative solutions, and overcome obstacles effectively.

SELF-EXPRESSION

Creativity is a powerful means of self-expression. Whether through art, writing, music, or other forms, it allows you to convey your thoughts, emotions, and ideas in a unique and personal way.

INNOVATION

Creativity is the foundation of innovation. It drives progress in various fields, from technology and science to business and the arts, leading to new inventions, products, and services.

BOOSTED CONFIDENCE

Accomplishing creative projects and seeing your ideas come to life can boost your self-confidence and sense of achievement.

JOY AND FULFILLMENT

Engaging in creative pursuits often brings joy and fulfillment. The process of creating and the sense of accomplishment from completing projects can lead to happiness.

COPING MECHANISM

Creativity can serve as a healthy coping mechanism during challenging times. It allows you to process emotions and find solace in creative expression.

DAY 25: EXPLORING CREATIVITY

INSPIRATION AND INNOVATION

Exposure to creative works, whether in the form of art, literature, music, or other media, can inspire and stimulate your own creativity, leading to fresh ideas and perspectives.

SELF-DISCOVERY

Creativity can lead to self-discovery by helping you uncover hidden talents, interests, and passions. It encourages introspection and a deeper understanding of yourself.

Overall, creativity enriches your life by promoting innovation, personal growth, self-expression, and well-being. Embracing creativity in your daily life, whether through artistic endeavors, problem-solving, or other creative outlets, can lead to a more fulfilling and meaningful existence.

Felicia's Grace Gems

REFERENCE SCRIPTURE | EXODUS 31:3-5 NIV

and I have filled him with the Spirit of God, with wisdom, with understanding, with knowledge and with all kinds of skills— 4 to make artistic designs for work in gold, silver and bronze, 5 to cut and set stones, to work in wood, and to engage in all kinds of crafts.

PRAYER POINT | CREATIVITY UNLEASHED

Ask God to help you tap into your inner creativity and to unlock the potential for artistic expression within you.

APPLICATION

Explore the role of creativity in your life. What creative outlets bring you joy and fulfillment.

DAY 26: DISCOVERING WHAT RESONATES WITH YOU

Finding a book, movie, or song that deeply resonates with you can be a personal and subjective experience. Here are steps to help you discover such a work and explain why it resonates with you:

REFLECT ON YOUR INTERESTS AND VALUES

Begin by reflecting on your interests, values, and experiences. What topics or themes resonate with you on a personal level? What are your passions and beliefs?

EXPLORE DIFFERENT GENRES AND MEDIUMS

Be open to exploring different genres and mediums. Don't limit yourself to just one type of entertainment. Try reading various genres of books, watching different types of movies, and listening to diverse music genres.

JOURNAL YOUR THOUGHTS

Keep a journal or digital notes where you record your thoughts and feelings about the work. Write about what aspects of the work connect with your personal experiences, values, or emotions.

EXPLORE DIFFERENT GENRES AND MEDIUMS

Be open to exploring different genres and mediums. Don't limit yourself to just one type of entertainment. Try reading various genres of books, watching different types of movies, and listening to diverse music genres.

EXPLORE YOUR INTERESTS

Start by exploring topics, genres, or themes that genuinely interest you. Look for content that aligns with your hobbies, passions, or values.

DAY 26: DISCOVERING WHAT RESONATES WITH YOU

REFLECT ON YOUR LIFE EXPERIENCES

Think about the experiences, challenges, and emotions you've encountered in your life. Look for content that mirrors those experiences or offers insights into them.

IDENTIFY WITH CHARACTERS

Pay attention to characters in books, movies, or songs. Is there a character whose struggles, personality traits, or journey resonates with your own life? Identify the aspects of their story that you relate to.

Ultimately, finding a book, movie, or song that deeply resonates with you is a personal journey that involves exploration, self-reflection, and openness to different forms of art and entertainment. When you find that special work that speaks to your soul, take the time to savor and appreciate the meaningful connection it brings to your life.

Felicia's Grace Gems

REFERENCE SCRIPTURE | 1 PETER 4:10-11 NIV

Each of you should use whatever gift you have received to serve others, as faithful stewards of God's grace in its various forms. If anyone speaks, they should do so as one who speaks the very words of God. If anyone serves, they should do so with the strength God provides, so that in all things God may be praised through Jesus Christ. To him be the glory and the power for ever and ever. Amen.

PRAYER POINT | WISDOM IN INTERPRETATION

Seek God's wisdom in interpreting and understanding the deeper meanings and messages within the content you encounter. Ask for discernment to grasp the intended lessons.

APPLICATION

Write about a book, movie, or song that has deeply resonated with you and explain why? What character do you relate to? How?

DAY 27: WHAT WILL YOU USE?

Women possess a diverse range of strengths that can be harnessed to overcome challenges in the world. Here are ways in which women can use their strengths to address and conquer various challenges:

RESILIENCE

Women often exhibit remarkable resilience in the face of adversity. They can use this strength to bounce back from setbacks and keep moving forward despite obstacles.

EMPATHY AND COMPASSION

Empathy and compassion are powerful tools for understanding and addressing societal challenges. Women can use these strengths to foster empathy in others and drive positive change.

COLLABORATION

Women excel at building and nurturing relationships. This strength can be instrumental in forming partnerships, coalitions, and support networks to tackle complex issues collectively.

ADVOCACY

Advocacy is a strength often exhibited by women. They can use their voices and influence to raise awareness, champion causes, and lobby for policy changes.

EMPOWERMENT OF OTHERS

Women often excel at empowering others to reach their full potential. This strength can be used to mentor, support, and uplift individuals facing challenges.

CULTURAL SENSITIVITY

Cultural sensitivity and awareness are strengths that can foster understanding and inclusivity, particularly in diverse and multicultural contexts.

DAY 27: WHAT WILL YOU USE?

CREATIVITY AND INNOVATION

Women can use their creativity and innovative thinking to develop novel approaches to longstanding challenges and drive progress in various sectors.

ADVANCING GENDER EQUALITY

Women can advocate for gender equality and empowerment, addressing issues such as gender-based violence, workplace discrimination, and unequal representation.

RESPECT FOR HUMAN RIGHTS

Upholding human rights, social justice, and equity are strengths that can guide efforts to combat discrimination and injustice.

Ultimately, women's strengths, combined with determination and collaboration, can drive positive change and create a more equitable and inclusive world. By recognizing and harnessing these strengths, women can contribute significantly to overcoming challenges and improving the well-being of individuals and communities.

Felicia's Grace Gems

REFERENCE SCRIPTURE | 1 CORINTHIANS 16:13 (NIV)

For we are God's handiwork, created in Christ Jesus to do good works, which God prepared in advance for us to do.

PRAYER POINT | OPPORTUNITIES FOR IMPACT

Pray for opportunities to make a meaningful impact in areas where your strengths can be most beneficial. Ask God to open doors and provide the right circumstances.

Imagine yourself as a character in a story. You are a powerful and resilient woman, describe your adventures and how you use your strengths to overcome challenges in the world?

Environmental Wellness

Hey Sis Hey,

Now it's time to talk about our surroundings and keeping the energy right around us. Being in tune with your environment and maintaining the purity of your surroundings is of upmost importance in maintaining growth. "Peaceful surroundings serve as a gentle balm for the soul, reminding us to slow down and savor the simple joys of life." - author unknown.

Your bond with the environment isn't just physical; it's an integral aspect of your identity. Consider it this way: we categorize individuals based on their surroundings, such as ' city girl' or ' country boy,' because there are elements of their environment intertwined with their behaviors.

Moment of reflection: A moment of self- reflection: What influence is my current environment exerting on my thoughts, feelings, and actions?

Be mindful of the environments you engage with, as they can significantly influence your well-being. Prioritize protecting your peace.

Situations, places, and relationships significantly affect your overall quality of life. The environments you expose yourself to can impact your well-being in various ways. Positive environments can create happiness, personal growth, and a sense of belonging, while negative ones can lead to stress, anxiety, and emotional turmoil. Similarly, the people you surround yourself with can either support and uplift you or contribute to stress and negativity.

In the same token of keeping relationships pure, maintaining cleanliness in your living spaces, car, and office can profoundly impact your mood and overall functioning. Many individuals with active lifestyles and young children can surely relate to me with the challenge of maintaining a clean car. Yet, the transformation when it's clean can make you feel rejuvenated. The environments you encounter do indeed affect your mood and aura, so safeguard your peace by creating clean and orderly spaces whenever possible. A clean and organized environment reduces stress, enhances focus, and uplifts your mood. It aids better concentration, productivity, and a sense of control.

In essence, the state of your surroundings directly influences your well-being, mentally and physically, making it essential to prioritize cleanliness in your daily life by taking ownership of your environment.

Gracefully submitted,

Felicia Willis

IGNITE THE FLAMES OF PASSION WITHIN YOU, AND YOUR RADIANCE WILL SERVE AS A BEACON OF INSPIRATION.

-F.E.W

DAY 28: ISOLATION ISN'T THAT BAD

Creating a peaceful and isolated environment can be beneficial for relaxation, reflection, and finding inner peace. Here are some tips to help you achieve a sense of peace in isolation:

CHOOSE THE RIGHT LOCATION

Find a quiet and secluded location that allows you to be away from noise and distractions. This could be a room in your home, a peaceful garden, a nearby park, or a natural setting like a forest or beach.

LIMIT TECHNOLOGY

Disconnect from digital devices and screens to reduce distractions and interruptions. Consider turning off your phone or putting it on silent mode.

SILENCE OR SOOTHING SOUNDS

Depending on your preference, you can choose complete silence or play soothing sounds such as nature recordings, gentle instrumental music, or white noise to create a peaceful atmosphere.

MINIMAL DECOR

Keep the space clutter-free and decorate it with items that promote tranquility, like candles, plants, or meaningful artwork.

BREATHING EXERCISES

Practice deep breathing exercises to help calm your mind and body. Focusing on your breath can be a powerful way to find peace in isolation.

MINDFULNESS AND MEDITATION

Engage in mindfulness or meditation practices to center your thoughts and reduce stress. These practices can help you become more present and peaceful.

READING AND CONTEMPLATION

Bring a book, poetry, or sacred texts that inspire you. Reading and contemplation can be a source of inner peace and spiritual growth.

DAY 28: ISOLATION ISN'T THAT BAD

SET BOUNDARIES

Communicate your need for isolation to those around you, and set boundaries to ensure you're not disturbed during your peaceful time.

ACCEPTANCE

Embrace the solitude and isolation as an opportunity for self-discovery and personal growth. Accept the present moment and find peace within it.

Remember that finding peace in isolation is a personal journey, and what works best for one person may differ from another. Explore these tips and customize them to suit your preferences and needs for tranquility and inner peace.

Felicia's Grace Gems

REFERENCE SCRIPTURE | MATTHEW 14:23 (NIV)
After he had dismissed them, he went up on a mountainside by himself to pray. Later that night, he was there alone.

PRAYER POINT | STILLNESS
Ask God to help you be still and fully present in the moment, allowing you to appreciate the tranquility of the place.

APPLICATION

Explore your favorite place of isolation and the sense of peace it brings to you.

DAY 29: DEVELOPING HABITS

Choosing a small daily habit that contributes to your overall well-being is a powerful way to improve your quality of life over time. Here's a step-by-step guide to help you pick and establish such a habit:

SELF-ASSESSMENT

Start by assessing your current well-being and identifying areas where you'd like to see improvement. Consider aspects like physical health, mental health, emotional well-being, relationships, and personal development.

BE SINCERE AND SPECIFIC

Define specific well-being goals you want to achieve. These goals should be realistic, measurable, and aligned with your values. For example, you might want to reduce stress, increase physical fitness, improve sleep quality, or enhance your social connections.

EMPHASIZE ROUTINE

Mention that this activity is a consistent part of your daily routine. Highlight the importance of consistency in nurturing your well-being.

ALIGNMENT WITH VALUES

Ensure that the activity aligns with your personal values and beliefs. Activities that resonate with your core values are more likely to be sustainable and fulfilling.

STAY ACCOUNTABLE

Share your commitment with a friend or family member who can help keep you accountable. Discuss your progress and challenges with them regularly.

DAY 29: DEVELOPING HABITS

SERVICE

Develop a habit of serving others. Seek out opportunities to volunteer and help those in need, both within and outside your church community.

Remember that the key to success is consistency and commitment. Small daily habits, when practiced consistently, can have a significant positive impact on your overall well-being and help you lead a healthier, happier life.

Felicia's Grace Gems

REFERENCE SCRIPTURE | 1 CORINTHIANS 6:19-20 NIV

Do you not know that your bodies are temples of the Holy Spirit, who is in you, whom you have received from God? You are not your own; you were bought at a price. Therefore honor God with your bodies.

PRAYER POINT | GUIDANCE

Pray for God's guidance and wisdom to help you choose the right daily activity for your well-being. Ask for discernment in recognizing what will benefit you the most.

APPLICATION

Describe a small daily activity that contributes to your overall well-being.

DAY 30: YOU'VE DONE THE WORK - NOW IT'S YOUR TURN!

Creating a women's empowerment group as a Christian woman can serve several meaningful purposes:

SPIRITUAL GROWTH

A women's empowerment group can provide a space for Christian women to grow spiritually together. Through prayer, Bible study, and discussions, members can deepen their faith and develop a stronger connection with God.

SUPPORT AND ENCOURAGEMENT

Women often face unique challenges and pressures. An empowerment group can offer emotional, mental, and spiritual support, allowing members to encourage and uplift one another during difficult times.

FELLOWSHIP AND COMMUNITY

Building a sense of community among Christian women can strengthen their relationships with one another and foster a sense of belonging. It's an opportunity to share life experiences, joys, and struggles.

PERSONAL DEVELOPMENT

Empowerment groups can focus on personal development and self-improvement. Members can set and pursue goals related to their faith, careers, relationships, and personal growth.

MENTORSHIP

Seasoned Christian women can serve as mentors to younger members, offering guidance, wisdom, and support in their spiritual journeys and life decisions.

PRAYER AND INTERCESSION

The group can engage in focused prayer and intercession for issues that concern women, their families, and their communities.

CULTIVATING GODLY VALUES

Women's empowerment groups can emphasize and reinforce godly values such as love, kindness, humility, and forgiveness

DAY 30: YOU'VE DONE THE WORK - NOW IT'S YOUR TURN!

BUILDING CONFIDENCE

Empowerment groups can help women build confidence in their abilities, talents, and contributions, encouraging them to step into leadership roles and make a positive impact.

The purpose of a women's empowerment group can vary based on the specific needs and goals of its members. Ultimately, it should align with Christian values and principles, nurturing spiritual growth, fostering community, and empowering women to live purposeful and fulfilling lives in accordance with their faith.

Felicia's Grace Gems

REFERENCE SCRIPTURE | TITUS 2:3-5 (NIV)

Likewise, teach the older women to be reverent in the way they live, not to be slanderers or addicted to much wine, but to teach what is good. Then they can urge the younger women to love their husbands and children, to be self-controlled and pure, to be busy at home, to be kind, and to be subject to their husbands so that no one will malign the word of God.

PRAYER POINT | PEACE

Pray for the strength and motivation to declutter and create a more peaceful environment

APPLICATION

If you could start a woman's focus group what would It be? Describe the vision, goals, and steps you would take to make It really?

Conclusion

Hey Sis Hey,

As you have followed this new journey, I hope you've found this experience as enriching as I have. We've journeyed together, experienced a range of emotions, learned, forgiven, and laughed.

Each letter was purposeful and crafted to assist you in unlocking your hidden capabilities. I hope the principles and lessons you've gained are deeply ingrained in your heart and life.

May this journal serve as a catalyst for positive change and transformation in your life. Remember, you have unique gifts to offer the world; be courageous in sharing them.

To all the women like me, juggling various roles, I pray that you prioritize self-care, set boundaries, and take breaks to recharge. Embrace your newfound boundaries and be intentional with setting your goals.

I've introduced my Wellness 365 concepts to you, and now it's your turn to shape your own vision of wellness moving forward. These remaining pages are yours to chart your path, to write, explore, create, process, and heal in your unique way. The upcoming days are dedicated to YOU! I hope you find joy in this, and don't hesitate to share your personal transformation story with others, showing them how God has impacted you on this journey. There's another sister looking up to you! Be the guiding light she needs to shine brightly.

Store this journal in a secure place so that in the years to come, you can return to it and measure your personal growth.

Gracefully submitted,

Felicia Willis